The Bald Eagle

by Judith Jango-Cohen

Lerner Publications Company • Minneapolis

To my friend Joyce Josephson, whose voice soars when she sings

Text copyright © 2003 by Judith Jango-Cohen

This book is available in two editions:
Library binding by Lerner Publications Company, a division of Lerner Publishing Group
Soft cover by First Avenue Editions, an imprint of Lerner Publishing Group
241 First Avenue North
Minneapolis, MN 55401 U.S.A.

Website address: www.lernerbooks.com

Words in **bold type** are explained in a glossary on page 31.

Library of Congress Cataloging-in-Publication Data

Jango-Cohen, Judith.
   The bald eagle / by Judith Jango-Cohen.
      p.   cm. — (Pull ahead books)
   Includes index.
   ISBN: 0–8225–3645–5 (lib. bdg. : alk. paper)
   ISBN: 0–8225–4750–3 (lib. pbk : alk. paper)
   1. United States—Seal—Juvenile literature. 2. Bald
eagle—Juvenile literature. 3. Emblems, National—United
States—Juvenile literature. 4. Animals—Symbolic aspects—
Juvenile literature. I. Title. II. Series.
   CD5610 .J36 2003
   929.9'2'0973—dc21   2002013950

Manufactured in the United States of America
1 2 3 4 5 6 – JR – 08 07 06 05 04 03

Do you have a bald eagle in your pocket?

If you have a dollar bill, you do. Bald eagles are on some coins, too. Why do we have bald eagles on our money?

The story begins in 1776. Americans were fighting for their freedom from England.

Americans did not want to be ruled by the English king. They wanted to be free to rule their own **nation**.

Their new nation became the United States of America.

Americans needed a **symbol** to stand for their new nation. Some nations had a dragon for their **national symbol**. Others had a lion.

The American leaders chose the **bald eagle** for their national symbol. Why do you think they chose the bald eagle?

The bald eagle is a proud-looking bird.

The United States was a proud new
nation. The eagle would show the
world how proud Americans felt.

Bald eagles are free to fly across the wide sky.

The bald eagle would be a symbol of a free new nation.

Bald eagles have strong wings and claws.

The United States would have to be
strong to stay free. The bald eagle
would stand for a strong, proud, and
free America.

Benjamin Franklin was one of America's
wisest leaders. He wished the bald
eagle had not been chosen.

The bald eagle steals fish from other birds, he said. It is a lousy and lazy bird. What symbol did Ben like better?

Ben Franklin thought the turkey would be a better symbol. But he did admit it was a silly bird.

Most Americans thought the bald eagle was a good national symbol. President George Washington even had eagles on his buttons.

In 1782, the eagle was placed on the
Great Seal of the United States.
The Great Seal is put on America's
important papers and letters.

The bald eagle is still our national symbol. But now it looks older and bolder. It stands for a bigger and stronger nation.

The **Presidential Seal** has an eagle on it, too. This seal stands for the **president** of the United States.

The eagle is also the symbol of the United States mail.

You may see eagles flying on flagpoles, buildings, and ships. One eagle even flew to the Moon!

This eagle was not a bird. It was an American **spacecraft** named the *Eagle*.

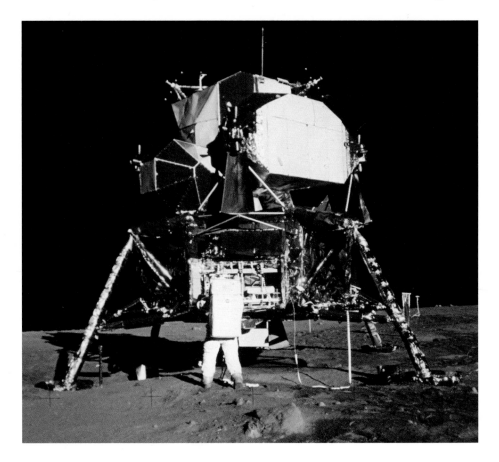

On July 20, 1969, this spacecraft
landed on the Moon. People on Earth
heard these proud words: "The *Eagle*
has landed."

The first American leaders never dreamed their eagle would be so proud, strong, and free.

Facts about the Bald Eagle

- Bald eagles are not bald. Their heads are covered by white feathers. The word "bald" also means "marked with white."

- Bald eagles have strong wings. They can fly as fast as cars drive on a highway. When they dive, they fly even faster.

- Bald eagles eat fish and small animals. They also eat dead animals. Sometimes bald eagles steal food from other animals. Maybe that's why Ben Franklin called them lousy and lazy.

- For hundreds of years, the bald eagle has been used as a symbol by Native Americans. Some see eagles as symbols of peace. They believe eagle feathers carry prayers to the Creator.

- The Nootka people tell of an eagle that can carry whales into the air. If the eagle drops the whale, we hear the sound as thunder.

Symbols on the Great Seal

Symbol	What It Stands For
13 red and white stripes........	first 13 states
13 olives and leaves.............	first 13 states
13 arrows........................	first 13 states
constellation of 13 stars........	nation of 13 states
olive branch......................	power to make peace
arrows	power to make war
blue..................................	justice
red..................................	courage
white..............................	purity

More about Bald Eagles

Books
Bernhard, Emery and Durga. *Eagles: Lions of the Sky.* New York: Holiday House, 1994.

Gibbons, Gail. *Soaring with the Wind: The Bald Eagle.* New York: William Morrow, 1998.

Johnson, Linda Carlson. *Our National Symbols.* Brookfield, CT: Millbrook Press, 1992.

Martin-James, Kathleen. *Soaring Bald Eagles.* Minneapolis: Lerner Publications Company, 2001.

Morrison, Gordon. *Bald Eagle.* Boston: Houghton Mifflin, 1998.

Websites
American Bald Eagle Information
  <http://www.baldeagleinfo.com>

Geobop's Symbols
  <http://www.geobop.com/symbols/index.htm>

The Great Seal of the United States
  <http://www.greatseal.com>

Where Bald Eagles Live
Bald eagles live only in North America. They live in open spaces near forests and water. Alaska, Florida, and the northern Mississippi River valley are three good places to see bald eagles.

Glossary

bald eagle: a large hunting bird. Adult bald eagles have white head feathers and white tail feathers.

Great Seal of the United States: the picture that stands for the United States of America. The seal is printed on America's important papers and letters.

nation: a country

national symbol: the picture that stands for a nation

president: the leader of a country, such as the United States

Presidential Seal: the picture that stands for the president of the United States

spacecraft: a machine that travels in space

symbol: an object that stands for an idea, a country, or a person

Index

Photo Acknowledgments

The pictures in this book have been reproduced with the permission of: © Harry M. Walker, pp. 3, 9, 10, 12, 14, 17, 18; © Judith Jango-Cohen, p. 4; North Wind Pictures, pp. 5, 6, 7, 8, 11, 13, 15, 16; Library of Congress, pp. 19, 21, 29; American Philosophical Society, p. 20; Corbis, pp. 22, 26; Eliot Cohen, pp. 23, 24; NASA, p. 25; Alan and Sandy Carey, p. 27.

Cover photo used with the permission of Alan and Sandy Carey.